Cutting Edge Careers in

ROBOTICS

Stuart A. Kallen

ReferencePoint
Press®

San Diego, CA

About the Author

Stuart A. Kallen is the author of more than 350 nonfiction books for children and young adults. He has written on topics ranging from the theory of relativity to the art of electronic dance music. In 2018, Kallen won a Green Earth Book Award from the Nature Generation environmental organization for his book *Trashing the Planet: Examining the Global Garbage Glut*. In his spare time, he is a singer, songwriter, and guitarist in San Diego.

For more information, contact:
ReferencePoint Press, Inc.
PO Box 27779
San Diego, CA 92198
www.ReferencePointPress.com

Picture Credits:

Cover: Gorodenkoff/Shutterstock
 6: Maury Aaseng
13: Suwin/Shutterstock.com
28: Hermdorff/Shutterstock.com
37: Monkey Business Images/Shutterstock.com
59: fizkes/Shutterstock.com
66: George Rudy/Shutterstock.com

LIBRARY OF CONGRESS CATALOGING-IN-PUBLICATION DATA

Names: Kallen, Stuart A., 1955- author.
Title: Cutting edge careers in robotics / by Stuart A. Kallen.
Description: San Diego, CA : ReferencePoint Press, 2020. | Series: Cutting
   edge STEM careers | Includes bibliographical references and index.
Identifiers: LCCN 2019051042 (print) | LCCN 2019051043 (ebook) | ISBN
   9781682828731 (library binding) | ISBN 9781682828748 (ebook)
Subjects: LCSH: Robotics--Vocational guidance.
Classification: LCC TJ211.25 .K35 2020 (print) | LCC TJ211.25 (ebook) |
   DDC 629.8/92023--dc23
LC record available at https://lccn.loc.gov/2019051042
LC ebook record available at https://lccn.loc.gov/2019051043

Contents

The Robot Revolution

Robotics are so well integrated into modern society as to be nearly invisible. Almost every consumer product, from baby powder to computers to cars, is manufactured by automated robotic hardware controlled by computer software. These robotic systems are designed, tested, and built by scientists and engineers with degrees in various fields including mechanics, robotics, artificial intelligence (AI), computing, and electronics. When the machines are up and running on factory floors, they are operated and maintained by technicians, programmers, and others who specialize in robotic processes.

The career field for robotics is experiencing unprecedented growth due to advances in engineering, artificial intelligence, and machine learning. This high-tech progress is converging to produce a new generation of automated machines that are increasingly smaller, cheaper, safer, and more easily programmed. With these advances, robots are expected to replace around 20 million workers globally by 2030, according to a 2019 analysis by the global forecasting firm Oxford Economics.

The increased reliance on robots will be bad news for some who work in manufacturing, food preparation, office administration, construction, agriculture, and commercial delivery and transportation. But the productivity benefits of automation are expected to boost economic growth. Analysts say this will result in more jobs being created than lost. And the robot revolution will be especially beneficial to engineers, technicians, programmers, scientists, and others who specialize in the field of robotics.

The Smart Factory

The Schneider Electric factory in Lexington, Kentucky, is considered a "smart factory" that exemplifies the way robots are transforming the manufacturing process. The facility makes fuse boxes and safety switches with automated lathes, drills, and metal press-es. Programmers write software code that provides instructions to machines that rivet, weld, paint, assemble, and test products. Workers trained as electromechanical technicians use augmented reality (AR)—overlaying digital information on an image of a real environment—to monitor the manufacturing equipment. The company's chief technology officer, Luke Durcan, describes the process: "You get a live feed from the [robot] to your smartphone or tablet. You know what the status [of the machine] is, whether it is running, whether there are any faults, alarms, or safety issues."[1] When problems pop up, technicians use the AR information to repair the robotic equipment.

Workers at Schneider share the factory floor with collaborative robots, or cobots. These advanced machines, which work alongside assemblers, function as mechanical arms that can tirelessly lift and move items as fast as they are produced. Built-in safety features prevent cobots from injuring human workers. And once workers leave for the day, the cobots continue to work in what is called lights-out mode. The robots function autonomously, or without human intervention, in the darkened factory, performing tests that have helped reduce the previous double-digit rejection rate caused by faulty assembly.

Cobots are increasingly relying on AI to function. Electronic sensors and machine-vision cameras located throughout the factory gather data from the manufacturing process. The data is analyzed by AI software, which extracts useful information. The information is analyzed and beamed to cobots and other robots that use it to learn how to operate more efficiently and navigate the factory floor without relying on a preprogrammed path. Designers are also utilizing AI to create new products. They can build a rough model and allow AI to instruct robots to generate manufacturing processes without human intervention.

Spectacular Growth

While traditional, low-skill assembly line workers are no longer needed in places like Schneider Electric, smart factories could not

Attributes That Matter to Employers

Written communication skills and the ability to solve problems are at the top of the list of attributes employers look for when considering new hires. This is the finding of a report titled "Job Outlook 2019." The report comes from the National Association of Colleges and Employers (NACE), an organization that surveys employers nationwide to learn more about their hiring plans in connection with recent college graduates. Other desirable attributes include the ability to work in a team setting, showing initiative, analytical skills, and a strong work ethic.

Attribute	% of Respondents
Communication skills (written)	82.0%
Problem-solving skills	80.9%
Ability to work in a team	78.7%
Initiative	74.2%
Analytical/quantitative skills	71.9%
Strong work ethic	70.8%
Communication skills (verbal)	67.4%
Leadership	67.4%
Detail oriented	59.6%
Technical skills	59.6%
Flexibility/adaptability	58.4%
Computer skills	55.1%
Interpersonal skills (relates well to others)	52.8%
Organizational ability	43.8%
Strategic planning skills	38.2%
Tactfulness	25.8%
Creativity	23.6%
Friendly/outgoing personality	22.5%
Entrepreneurial skills/risk-taker	16.9%
Fluency in a foreign language	11.2%

Source: "Job Outlook 2019," NACE, November 2018.
www.odu.edu/content/dam/odu/offices/cmc/docs/nace/2019-nace-job-outlook-survey.pdf.

exist without a workforce trained in robotics. Manufacturing engineers design the automated assembly systems that are in high demand. Robotics engineers develop sensors and other hardware, while data scientists work to develop AR and AI machine-learning software.

As e-commerce giants like Amazon move to increase their use of robots to fulfill orders, those who specialize in robotics will remain in high demand. An analysis by news site Business Wire predicts over 4 million commercial robots will be installed in over 50,000 warehouses by 2025, up from around 4,000 robotic warehouses in 2018. With this spectacular growth, average salaries for robotics specialists are some of the highest of any tech field, ranging from $83,000 to $136,000 annually. And according to the Bureau of Labor Statistics (BLS), robotics and AI job postings are surging with double- and triple-digit increases seen every year. With a global robotics market expected to attract nearly $150 billion in revenue by 2025, a career in robotics is a career with a future.

Electromechanical Technician

What Does an Electromechanical Technician Do?

Most clothing is comparatively cheap because it is made by poorly paid workers in developing nations like Bangladesh and Vietnam. But in 2019, a new kind of clothing factory opened in Arkansas, meant to compete with low-cost foreign labor. The TY Garments factory in Little Rock utilizes twenty-four sewing robots called Sewbots. Each Sewbot produces a T-shirt in about thirty seconds and can run twenty-four hours a day. TY Garments is expected to employ 400 people, but they will not be sewing T-shirts according to Raj Rajan, chief executive of Soft-Wear Automation, which designed the Sewbots: "We want people who can work with robots."[2]

Rajan says most of the new jobs will go to technicians with electromechanical knowledge. These specialists keep the robots humming at maximum efficiency. Electromechanical technicians have a detailed understanding of the metal, plastic, and electronic components that make up robotic machinery, and they use their knowledge of mechanical systems and electronics to test and maintain the automated equipment.

Electromechanical technicians work primarily with the three basic robotic components. Computer chips are the

---

A Few Facts

Number of Jobs
14,000 in 2018

Pay
$57,790 median annual salary in 2018

Educational Requirements
Associate degree

Personal Qualities
Aptitude for math, mechanically inclined, problem solver

Work Settings
Factory floors, computer control rooms, workshops

Future Job Outlook
3.5 percent growth through 2026

robot brains that control various mechanical parts like motors, pistons, grippers, wheels, and gears that move, grab, turn, and lift. These mechanical parts are propelled by pneumatic (air) systems and hydraulic (fluid) systems that are maintained by electromechanical technicians. Electromechanical technicians also test, adjust, and replace the variety of sensors and cameras that allow a robot to "see" and "hear." These sensors determine the size and shape of materials, the space between objects, and other details of the robot's physical surroundings.

Sometimes electromechanical technicians are called on to put together an assembly line made up of robotic equipment. This requires them to follow blueprints, schematics, and electric diagrams, instructions that provide details about setting up machines and other pieces of equipment. The technicians work with precision electronic measuring instruments to ensure robots are functioning properly. If replacement parts are needed, a technician might use metalworking machinery and power tools to create housings, fittings, and fixtures used in hydraulic, pneumatic, and other systems.

Electromechanical technicians use soldering equipment and hand tools to test, repair, and install circuit boards, connectors, and other electronic parts. Repairs often take place when the robot itself notifies an electromechanical technician. Robotics technician Camden West explains, "Most robots will sound an alarm and identify what that alarm means. For example, it might tell you one of the circuit boards is bad. It will give you the exact description of what's wrong and how to fix it. Sometimes that's as easy as going into maintenance mode and resetting the memory."[3]

Large factories often use hundreds of robots. This requires electromechanical technicians to work as specialists, focusing on a particular process or piece of equipment. And the learning process never stops. Maintenance superintendent Chuck Mastriania says, "Even for a seasoned [technician] it takes five to six years until they feel comfortable working by themselves, if necessary, and they still won't know everything at that point."[4]

A Typical Workday for Electromechanical Technicians

Robotic factories can only work when all the various pieces of an assembly line are trouble free and operating at maximum efficiency. Most electromechanical technicians work in offices, in control rooms, and on factory floors carefully monitoring equipment to ensure it is operating smoothly. They use test instruments like oscilloscopes, voltmeters, and software applications to examine mechanical and electronic processes. They are required to keep detailed documentation of test results. Some of the work involves physical inspection of robotic parts to ensure mechanisms are not cracked, deteriorating, or otherwise defective. Technicians also inspect finished products made by robots to locate flaws.

Electromechanical technicians need to be team players. They attend meetings and work alongside mechanical and electrical engineers, supervisors, and assembly-line workers. Like workers in most fields, technicians talk on the phone, text, and use email on a daily basis. And as electromechanical contractor Kara Powers explains, many work hours are spent in front of a laptop computer: "I remember when we used to have to carry around a pile of books, just like the college kids, except ours were way bigger. Taking a laptop with you is way easier, and you can get all the manuals and information and help you need without walking all over the place and looking through books. Having everything in hand is much more efficient."[5]

Education and Training

Many jobs in robotics require an advanced degree in computer science, data science, or engineering, but most who work as electromechanical technicians need only a two-year associate degree. Associate degrees in electromechanical technology can be obtained at community colleges, vocational-technical schools, and extension divisions of colleges and universities. The Accreditation Board for Engineering and Technology (ABET) certifies all associate degree programs for electromechanical technicians that require college-level algebra, trigonometry, and basic science courses.

High school students interested in pursuing an associate degree to become an electromechanical technician should focus on math, science, drafting, and computer classes. Technicians in this field work often with tools and machinery, so courses in automotive repair or metal fabrication can also be beneficial.

Skills and Personality

Having mechanical skills and an aptitude for math are important for aspiring electromechanical technicians. Math is used every day to make and record precise measurements, operate high-tech equipment, and analyze problems. Mechanical skills come into play when techs remove or install small parts and fix equipment. Electromechanical technicians are skilled in reading detailed diagrams and blueprints for circuit boards, processors, chips, and other electronics. They have highly developed computer skills that allow them to understand many types of software used to control, test, and design equipment.

Communication skills are also valued because electromechanical technicians must be able to understand directions and communicate problems with engineers and team leaders. Many techs work directly with clients and need to develop customer relationship skills. Field service technician Brian Lentz asserts, "[Customer relationship skills are] equal to or more important than the technical side. You can be the smartest guy in the room, but if you can't get along with the customer, they're not going to come back. What's more, a critical skill is the ability to do troubleshooting over the phone, without actually seeing the equipment. That, too, is part of keeping the customer happy."[6]

Electromechanical technicians also need to stay on top of changes in the industry and advancements in technology. Critical-thinking abilities are imperative when evaluating systems, troubleshooting glitches, and finding answers to problems. As automation technician Kenneth Mainville explains,

The biggest thing is to think out of the box [and] have an open mind. It can be stressful when the customer is on you to resolve something right away, and sometimes the automation is something you've never seen before. You might have to recreate in your mind how something works so you can understand how the problem happened in the first place.[7]

Working Conditions

Electromechanical technicians spend their days in loud, dangerous industrial environments and are often required to wear safety equipment including hard hats, goggles, ear protection, and steel-toed boots. Depending on where they work, electromechanical technicians might be exposed to injury from electrical equipment, automated machinery, excessive dust and heat, toxic fumes, and hazardous materials.

While most electromechanical technicians work in manufacturing centers, some work outdoors. They might test, maintain, and repair unmanned submarines used in oil drilling or deep-sea exploration, or work on robotic equipment used in forestry, mining, or agriculture. Other electromechanical technicians specialize

in wind turbines. They spend their workdays repairing equipment that might be 300 feet (91 m) above the ground. These jobs involve travel and spending days away from home, including holidays and weekends.

Employers and Pay

In 2019, *USA Today* listed forty-three of the highest paying jobs a person can get with an associate degree. With an annual salary of $57,790 in 2018, electromechanical technician came in at number twenty-one. Those who work in this field are in demand because companies are increasingly relying on robotics to produce complex electronics, medical equipment, military goods, and countless other products.

Robots have also become essential tools in heavy industry such as steel and gas production and waste management. As Doug Putnam-Pite, who develops software for automated assembly lines, explains, "While the repetitive and dangerous jobs are being replaced by robots, the irony is that these same factories will now need highly trained technicians . . . to service and maintain these new robots and automation."[8]

What Is the Future Outlook for Electromechanical Technicians?

Since the late 1990s, millions of jobs have moved offshore to developing nations where labor is cheap. But an increasing number of companies are finding that robots allow them to remain competitive while keeping production facilities in the United States. And more companies are upgrading their production facilities every day to accommodate robotic technology. This means that people trained as electromechanical technicians will see an increase in job opportunities well into the future. While the BLS predicts that that the field will only grow by 3.5 percent through 2026, this statistic is based on an analysis of traditional manufacturers like car makers where demand is flat.

With robots taking on new roles in gaming, education, aerospace, agriculture, marine technology, and elsewhere, those who specialize in testing and maintaining cutting-edge robotic equipment can expect to be in greater demand than the BLS projects. As technical marketing engineer Bill Dehner says,

> From automated manufacturing to self-driving cars and vacuum cleaners, robots and machines have infiltrated and will continue to infiltrate our everyday lives. . . . The future of automation holds a lot of exciting opportunities and career possibilities.[9]

Find Out More

Accreditation Board for Engineering and Technology (ABET)

www.abet.org

ABET accredits college and university programs in applied science, computing, engineering, and engineering technology at the associate's, bachelor's, and master's degree levels. The organization's website provides lists of ABET-accredited programs, information about attaining accreditation, and links to information about workshops and scholarships.

Automation Federation

www.automationfederation.org

This organization is dedicated to advancing the science and engineering of automation technologies applied to manufacturing, cybersecurity, and infrastructure. The group's website features webinars, research and white papers, and educational materials about robotics and automation.

Modern Materials Handling

www.mmh.com

Modern Materials Handling has been covering the automated manufacturing industry since 1946. Its website features articles about technology and equipment of interest to anyone pursuing a career as an electromechanical technician. Website resources include white papers, webcasts, and special reports concerning robotics, software, and automation.

Technology Student Association

https://tsaweb.org

The Technology Student Association is open to middle and high school students enrolled in or who have completed technology education courses. Members work on competitive events, develop leadership skills, and attend conferences. The association offers members scholarships, access to apprenticeship programs, and counseling by industry advisors.

Robotics Programmer

What Does a Robotics Programmer Do?

Robots can do amazing things, from assembling cars to driving those cars down the road. While robots accomplish this work with an intricate mix of gears, pistons, switches, motors, and sensors, a robot's hardware is only as good as the software that tells it what to do. Technology journalist Alex Salkever writes, "Robots are just software in a hardware skin."[10] The robot's software "brain" is created by a robotics programmer. This specialist, sometimes called a roboticist, writes lines of computer code that instruct hardware to perform tasks, interpret sounds and sights, and safely move objects.

Robotics programmers play an essential role in modern industrial innovation. Robots are a mainstay of many manufacturing processes, and the job has become more complex with the advent of sensor-rich robots that can learn ever more complicated tasks. Although robotics programmers possess specialized knowledge, they conduct many tasks that are basic to all computer programming. Robotics programmers design, write, test, debug, and maintain the source code of computer programs. As robotics engineer Brian Feldman explains, "Many of the programming concepts and topics that are important in robotics—such as artificial intelligence, data abstraction, user interface design, decision making, and security, to name a few—are actually not just specific to robotics, but are present in many non-robotic applications as well."[11] Beyond the basics, those who program robots understand the AI and machine learning programs that enable a robot to improve its abilities without human intervention.

Writing code and applications for robotic equipment is called off-line programming—it is done on a computer and later uploaded to the robotic equipment. A second method of programming, called on-line programming, involves physically moving a robot through a series of actions using what is called a teach pendant. The teach pendant is a control that looks something like a handheld gaming device with buttons, dials, and a color touchscreen. To program a robot's actions, the operator moves the robot from place to place using buttons on the pendant. Each motion or position of the robot can be saved on the pendant. After the entire range of movements has been stored, the robot can autonomously re-create the actions at a rapid rate.

A Typical Workday

Robotics programmers work in offices alongside managers, research scientists, and engineers who specialize in sales, manufacturing, and robotics. When a company wants to bring a new robotic product, like an automated vacuum cleaner or drone, to market, programmers are involved in every step of the process. Robotics programmers work on product development, prototype testing, production supervision, and debugging finished products. Those who work with robotic assembly lines install, maintain, and update automated equipment. They analyze drawings and blueprints and might be called upon to physically set up and place robots in the workspace.

Education and Training

High school students interested in becoming robotics programmers should take as many math courses as possible, including calculus, trigonometry, and algebra. Computer science courses that emphasize programming languages are helpful. Popular coding languages in robotics include Python and C++. Motivated students can teach themselves the basics of programming. Software engineer Chris Loy offers:

> My main piece of advice is simply to get coding! If you have a computer and internet access then you can start teaching yourself for free. Find an online course, build a cool website, solve some coding puzzles and get started. It's important to take an interest in tech as well. Podcasts are good, although I prefer tech blogs personally. Look for articles that have code in them or link to a GitHub repository and then play around with the code.[12]

Those planning a career in robotics programming can also attend coding boot camps. These twenty-four-week courses, which are usually open to high school students, teach coding and career development. Some robotics programmers began their careers as kids, building and programming their own robots. Rodney Brookes, who founded iRobot, the company that makes Roomba vacuums, built his first robot when he was twelve.

In addition to understanding coding languages backwards and forwards, robotics programmers need to be skilled in the use of two software applications. Robotics Operating System (ROS) is a set of software tools and libraries for obtaining, building, writing, and running code across multiple computers. ROS is open source, which means it can be downloaded for free. ROS is similar to commercial robot frameworks such as Player and Microsoft Robotics Studio. A second open-source programming platform, Matlab, is used to analyze data and develop algorithms for machine learning applications.

Most robotics programmers hold a bachelor of computer science degree, commonly referred to as a CS degree. They take math-heavy courses in computer programming, algorithms, data structures, logic and computation, calculus, linear algebra, and statistics. Other courses focus on operating systems, real-time computing, artificial intelligence, machine learning, and software testing.

Many companies offer summer intern positions to computer science students who are studying robotics programming. Candidates work with teams in a fast-moving environment to integrate, deploy, and support complex software systems. Interns participate in research and development, problem solving, maintenance, and other tasks. To qualify for internships, candidates are required to be enrolled in a college or university, and they must be familiar with various robotics operating systems, installation procedures, coding, and process management.

Skills and Personality

Writing and analyzing computer code hour after hour—and relating to clients and other workers—requires technical talents and what are called soft skills or people skills. On the technical side,

Hands-on Robot Programming

"The hard part of robot programming isn't writing the basic code that makes the robot work. Rather, it's observing what the robot actually does when it executes that code, figuring out why it doesn't behave the way you expected, and then changing things to make it work better—or maybe at all. After a large number of iterations [repetitions], the structure of the code may be quite similar to what you started with but the details are usually very different. . . . Subtlety and great complexity characterize the interaction between robots and the real world. Mastering the programming that connects the two requires hands-on experience."

—Joe Jones, robotics programmer

Quoted in Hope Reese, "The Next Big Job in Tech: Robot Programmer," TechRepublic, November 28, 2016. www.techrepublic.com.

robotics programmers need strong math and programming skills so that writing code becomes second nature. The ability to concentrate on extremely complex lines of code for long periods of time is also necessary along with an eye for detail; even the slightest error can result in a robot performing poorly or breaking down. An analytical mindset is useful for problem solving.

Good communication skills are a must, since robotics programmers work with developers, engineers, managers, and others. Good communication means expressing complex ideas clearly in plain English and listening closely to the comments, suggestions, and questions posed by others. Communication extends to writing; robotics programmers are required to publish weekly progress reports and other documents. And the old saying "patience is a virtue" is especially true for robotics programmers. Production lines are constantly updated and retooled. Robotics programmers need to be calm and supportive while working on what might seem like a never-ending process.

Successful robotics programmers need to adapt rapidly to change. Technology moves very fast, and programmers often need to update their skills and quickly learn new concepts and techniques. Perhaps the most difficult skill to pick up is learning to think like a robot; as programmer Alex Owen-Hill explains:

> It's not your skills in advanced mathematics; it's not your ability to code ultra-efficient algorithms; and it's not even your familiarity with programming languages (although obviously these can all be quite helpful). When programming physical robots, one thing is often far more important. Great robot programmers are able to comprehend how the robot perceives the world, and program effectively within the robot's limitations.[13]

Working Conditions

The work culture at most companies that specialize in robotics is demanding. Robotics programmers begin their days going through emails from team members who need guidance or who have discovered problems with an application. When writing code, programmers need to remain focused on minute details for long periods of time. On a typical workday, a robotics programmer might test, maintain, and monitor computer programs; review and scrutinize computer printouts to locate code problems; and develop new programs.

Teamwork is important as robotics programmers are called upon to solve problems for less experienced staff, attend management meetings, and work with engineers to expand or modify systems. Phil Mass, who developed the original Roomba software, emphasizes that teamwork can provide solutions to thorny problems. "From my experience, some problems in robotics can only be solved by a clever combination of software, electronics and mechanical design," Mass says. "Make sure all of your [developers] are working closely together and are talking to each other about their problems. Sometimes a solution can come from an unexpected direction."[14]

Employers and Pay

Robotics programmers work in a variety of industries dominated by automation and robotics. In 2019 robotics programmer jobs were being offered by major automobile producers, aerospace companies, makers of medical equipment, and manufacturers of robotic assembly lines. The online retailer Amazon is installing robots that carry heavy pallets and move products from place to place in its massive warehouses. The construction equipment company Caterpillar is developing cutting-edge construction robots, including a brick-laying robot called Hadrian X which can lay one thousand bricks an hour. In agriculture, John Deere is working to develop robotics tractors that spray fertilizers and pick crops using machine vision and artificial intelligence. And these are just a few of the employers that are eager to hire robotics programmers and willing to pay them well. While the average American worker earned around $47,000 in 2019, the average annual salary for robotics programmers was $83,241, according to jobs website Glassdoor.

What Is the Future Outlook for Robotics Programmers?

The BLS defines robotics programmers as software developers, and this job sector is expected to experience exceptional growth. According to the BLS, demand for software developers will grow 21 percent through 2028.

Find Out More

Codecademy
www.codecademy.com

This online school offers free coding lessons in numerous programming languages, including Python, C++, Git, JavaScript, and CSS. Students can sign up and begin coding within minutes.

National Robotics Education Foundation (NREF)

www.the-nref.org

The NREF is dedicated to the goal of providing robotics education curricula in elementary, middle, and high schools. The foundation's website provides curricula and lesson programs, a robotics education journal, and links to related robotics websites.

Software Development Forum (SD Forum)

www.sdforum.org

The SD Forum is based in the Silicon Valley and holds around twenty-five events monthly that are attended by engineers, developers, entrepreneurs, and technology experts. The forum provides information, education, and connections to those seeking to build a career in the Silicon Valley.

TopCoder

www.topcoder.com

This website with nearly one million highly skilled members hosts bimonthly computer programming contests where software developers, designers, and student programmers compete for cash prizes while solving coding problems.

Manufacturing Engineer

What Does a Manufacturing Engineer Do?

If you love the smartphone, video game console, microwave snacks, and other mass-produced goodies in your home, you can thank manufacturing engineers. These professionals design the automated production lines that act as the backbone of the manufacturing process. As manufacturing engineer Andy Orin explains, "Manufacturing engineers create plans and instructions that detail exactly how to build hardware with the tools and machinery out on the [factory] floor. Think LEGO instructions, but a lot more complex."[15] Orin works in electronics manufacturing, which utilizes a web of complex, computer-driven, automated assembly lines. The equipment on an assembly line might include robotic arms, welders, paint sprayers, circuit board printers, conveyor belts, employee workstations, and sensors that allow machines to "see" and "feel" tiny components.

In addition to creating assembly lines, manufacturing engineers program each machine to do exactly what it is supposed to do in coordination with the other machines. Engineers also create software programs that guide the actions of the entire assembly line. The machines must work in harmony twenty-four hours a day while repeatedly producing thousands of identical products in a seamless, efficient manner. This is demanding work—each machine must move very precisely or chaos will ensue. As manufacturing engineer Becky Miller states, "An error the size of a human hair can make a difference."[16]

Engineers who specialize in manufacturing spend time researching and testing new equipment that might make their assembly line more efficient and cost effective. If a new machine or system looks promising, the engineer will conduct what is called a return on investment (ROI) analysis. The engineer evaluates the machinery, determines its quality and efficiency, and decides if the benefits outweigh the purchase costs.

While the main focus of manufacturing engineers is on equipment and processes, there is a human factor to consider. Manufacturing engineers work closely with laborers and offer support on the factory floor. Orin says, "Fabricators (hourly laborers) who work on hardware (our products) come to us with any questions or problems they might have: issues with their machinery, issues with the hardware, questions on work instructions, basically anything. Manufacturing engineers solve the problems on the floor to keep product moving."[17]

In addition to their other duties, manufacturing engineers fill out forms and production reports. They create and review schedules, engineering specifications, safety records, environmental requirements, and budgets. When paperwork reveals glitches, such as a high number of rejected products, manufacturing engineers devise and test new quality control procedures to minimize problems.

A Typical Workday

Joe Dyer is a manufacturing engineer who works on the tech solutions team at DISHER, which produces assembly line equipment. Dyer says his work life revolves around three major components: working with operators, operations, and opportunities.

His interaction with operators consists of developing relationships with customers, instructing engineers on factory floors, and listening to the suggestions of line operators who work with the equipment.

On the operations front, manufacturing engineers keep an intense focus on the numerous processes that need to come together to produce a product. Dyer lists some of the operations he oversees:

> The process of receiving shipments of raw materials; the process of moving material within a plant . . . the process of assembly; and the process of shipping. . . . You get the point. Manufacturing follows a process. You need to know the process. The best manufacturing engineers have a deep appreciation for the processes that govern their day.[18]

Most manufacturers have entire departments devoted to each specific process. Engineers spend their days pulling together the needs and desires of each department into a cohesive production strategy.

Dyer views solving problems as an opportunity to make things better in the long run. He says some problems are easy to solve. Others can be spotted quickly but might be difficult to fix. Still other problems are hard to find and harder to fix. Whatever the case, finding solutions presents an opportunity to save his employer money and avoid bigger problems in the future.

Education and Training

Manufacturing engineers are required to have a bachelor of science degree in engineering. They might major in mechanical engineering, industrial engineering, electrical engineering, manufacturing engineering, or industrial engineering technology. Elizabeth Walker, a General Motors manufacturing engineer, describes her education:

I received my Bachelor's degree in mechanical engineering from Cornell University. Studying mechanical engineering gave me important problem solving and critical thinking skills that have allowed me to explore a variety of engineering disciplines and varying career opportunities. Then, while working full time, I . . . received a Master's degree in manufacturing engineering.[19]

Math is the foundation for all engineering studies, and students should take as many math courses as possible. General math teaches students to think in logical ways, algebra is useful for creating algorithms while writing software, and geometry is used when creating plans and blueprints. Manufacturing technology, which uses electricity, mechanics, heat, light, sound, and optics, is based on applied physics. This means prospective manufacturing engineers should attend physics classes where they will learn to grasp how circuits, processors, and other components function.

College coursework for manufacturing engineering majors includes classes in statistics, production systems planning, and manufacturing systems design. Some colleges and universities offer five-year degree programs that provide students with a

Fast-Paced Fun

"Manufacturing engineering as a discipline is not just about keeping the line moving. It's much broader than that. On any given day in the life of an engineer in manufacturing, I am expected to provide expertise in: manufacturing processes, quality tools, industrial engineering, automation technologies, design . . . process development, and continuous improvement. These areas of expertise are applied in various degrees at every company but each facet is present at any successful manufacturer. The modern manufacturing plant is high tech, fast paced, and innovative. This is exactly what makes manufacturing appealing to me and positively fun."

—Joe Dyer, manufacturing engineer

Joe Dyer, "A Day in the Life of a Manufacturing Engineer," DISHER, August 17, 2017. https://disher.com.

bachelor's and a master's degree. Coursework might include systems engineering, computer system security foundations, probability for electrical engineers, broadband network architectures, and modern active circuit design.

Skills and Personality

Dyer says manufacturing engineers need expertise in many fields, but success comes down to three core disciplines: "a passion for people, an understanding of the process, and a knack for problem solving."[20] Understanding processes requires manufacturing engineers to possess strong operational skills, which help them operate efficiently on a day-to-day basis. Attention to detail is an operational skill especially important in the manufacturing field. Engineers work with intricate parts and search for the tiniest glitches in the automation process. The need for problem-solving requires engineers to have an eye for detail when examining physi-

A manufacturing engineer tests software. These engineers program machines to work in coordination with other machines and spend time researching and testing new equipment that might make machines more efficient and cost effective.

cal machinery or lines of computer code. And they also need to be patient and persistent when solving problems. Multitasking skills are important for manufacturing engineers who need to remain organized and focused while simultaneously dealing with puzzling plans, tiny pieces of hardware, and demands from production managers and chief executive officers (CEOs).

A manufacturing engineer also must possess what are called soft skills, those abilities that allow the engineer to work well with others. This might mean patiently explaining a new technique to a laborer or trying to convince a manager to change manufacturing processes. Becky Miller claims, "My job is actually very people-oriented. I work with groups of people every day to resolve problems. To get everyone to work together on a problem, typically I like to make sure everybody agrees that there is a problem."[21]

Manufacturing engineers who work at big companies or for the government are not required to have a special license. However, those who are seeking a higher level of leadership, with a commensurate level of pay, can benefit from obtaining a professional engineer (PE) license. This requires the engineer to pass a Fundamentals of Engineering exam, work under a licensed PE for four years, and then take a Principles and Practice of Engineering exam.

Working Conditions

In factories that run twenty-four hours a day, manufacturing engineers might work in shifts. Typically, employees on the first shift work from 6:00 a.m. to 3:00 p.m. The second shift runs from 3:00 p.m. until 12:00 a.m., while the third shift overlaps the second, from 10:00 p.m. to 6:00 a.m. The hours worked by manufacturing engineers vary depending on the company. Some work double shifts three or four days a week; some work one shift five or six days. Manufacturing engineers may work the same shift all the time, or they may be asked to rotate. They might also be required to work on weekends and holidays. While shift work can be a grind, Elizabeth Walker loves her job. "Every day as a manufacturing engineer is different. I am constantly working to resolve

Building GM Trucks

"In my role as a manufacturing engineer, I design and build the tooling and system required for building our vehicles at General Motors. Last year I led a project to transform an SUV plant into a truck plant in six months. During the six months of converting the plant, I worked to design and build tools that are used to install parts to the truck; I worked with construction companies to get equipment installed, and I worked with plant operators to refine processes and problem solve any issues with building the vehicle."

—Elizabeth Walker, manufacturing engineer

Elizabeth Walker, "A Day in the Life of Manufacturing Engineer Elizabeth Walker," All Together, March 11, 2019. https://alltogether.swe.org.

issues so that we can build the world's best vehicles. I love that every day has new challenges and problems to solve," she says. "The manufacturing environment is fast-paced and the problems we solve need quick solutions so that we are providing the best product to the customer. . . . It's very rewarding."[22]

Employers and Pay

The BLS places manufacturing engineers in the same category as industrial engineers who earned an average salary of $87,470 in 2018. However, according to the BLS, engineers who work in transportation manufacturing earned several thousand dollars more per year, while those who specialized in computer and electronics manufacturing earned on average $93,760 in 2018.

What Is the Future Outlook for Manufacturing Engineers?

Manufacturing engineers work in a wide range of industries that produce consumer products. As more companies retool with new robotic equipment, engineers who specialize in manufacturing, research, and development are expected to remain in high demand. According to the BLS, employment of all industrial engineers is expected to grow by 8 percent through 2028, slightly faster than the average 7 percent for all occupations.

Find Out More

American Society for Engineering Education (ASEE)
www.asee.org

The ASEE advances the development of innovative approaches to engineering education. The "Education & Careers" link on the society's website offers webinars, courses and workshops, and information about academic job opportunities.

Engineering Education Service Center
www.engineeringedu.com

This website provides links to many resources for future engineers, including a Summer Camp Directory, an Engineering Scholarship Directory, a Competition Directory, and the Women in Engineering Program Directory. The site also sells books, DVDs, and other products used by engineering students.

Institute of Industrial & Systems Engineers (IISE)
www.iise.org

The IISE is made up of engineering professionals who work in automobile manufacturing, aerospace, heath care, education, and other fields. The institute publishes blogs, white papers, and newsletters, and offers training, scholarships, and career advice for young professionals.

Society of Manufacturing Engineers (SME)
www.sme.org

The SME was founded to promote manufacturing technology, attract future engineers, and develop a skilled workforce. The SME Educational Foundation offers training, scholarships, contests and competitions, student summits, and mentorships with professional engineers.

Robotics Engineer

A Few Facts

Number of Jobs
312,000 in 2018*

Pay
$87,370 median annual salary in 2018*

Educational Requirements
Bachelor of science degree in engineering

Personal Qualities
Team player, good communication skills, lifelong learner

Work Settings
Offices, drafting rooms, factory floors, and field work

Future Job Outlook
4 percent growth through 2018*

* For all mechanical engineers

What Does a Robotics Engineer Do?

In 2019, Stevie went to work in the Knollwood Military Retirement Community in Washington, DC. Stevie performs a number of jobs at the retirement community, including taking food orders and helping seniors contact doctors and family members. Stevie carries on conversations, reminds seniors to take their medicines, plays games, tells jokes, calls out bingo numbers, and leads group karaoke sessions. While some of the seniors are a little put off by Stevie, others are fascinated by the 4-foot-7-inch (1.3 m) robot equipped with autonomous navigation and a face that doubles as a video-conferencing screen.

Stevie is an assistive robot created in Ireland by robotics engineer Connor McGuinn. McGuinn states:

Seniors enjoyed interacting with Stevie. It being so expressive helped to humanize the technology in a way that surpassed our expectations. These insights lead us to believe that a robot like Stevie can have a wide range of high-impact uses, which may involve performing numerous assistive tasks, helping caregivers, and may even provide new interfaces to existing technologies—like video calling, smart sensors, social media—that can be inaccessible to many older adults.[23]

The field of robotics is evolving rapidly, and the tasks performed by robotics engineers range from the routine to the visionary, depending on where they work. Those who are employed by manufacturers might design and test new robots for production lines, while others monitor and maintain older installations that are used every day. Some robotics engineers spend most of their time conducting pure research. They use their knowledge to design experimental robots like Stevie that might someday make up for the growing shortage of caregivers and health care workers.

Whatever task a robotics engineer is assigned to, the work is multidisciplinary. This means robotics combines several different academic disciplines that focus on mechanical, electronic, and computerized systems. Robotics engineers use mechanical engineering skills to design a robot's moving hardware, which includes bearings and actuators. (An actuator is the tiny electrical motor and gearbox that drives a robot's joints.) A robot's wiring, control devices, power systems, and sensors require knowledge of electronics engineering. And those who create a robot's processor, programs, and AI systems have knowledge of computer and software engineering. Then there is the esoteric field of kinematics. This mathematical discipline, sometimes called the geometry of motion, focuses on the position, velocity, and acceleration of objects and groups of objects. While few robotics engineers are experts in all of these fields, they work in teams and combine their knowledge to create sophisticated robotic machinery.

A Typical Workday

Robotics engineers work in offices, in drafting studios, and on factory floors. They spend many hours in front of computers writing

Writing Code, Printing Parts

"Every day is different. I spend a lot of time writing code, C++, Java and some Python and PHP (Hypertext Preprocessor) occasionally. . . . Sometimes I'll spend all day drawing software architecture onto a sketch pad as I wonder about how [robots] think. When I'm doing this type of work I'm in my office in comfortable clothes. I spend a lot of time drawing things in CAD. . . . Frequently I print 3D parts or cast aluminum parts from 3D printed designs. . . . I'm usually in overalls wearing ear and eye protection as I stand over the loud equipment and monitor the progress."

—Cagney Moreau, robotics engineer

Cagney Moreau, "What Does a Robotics Engineer's Day-to-Day Job Look Like?," Quora, April 13, 2019. www.quora.com.

code and designing robotic machinery. This generally requires them to use two types of software programs, computer-aided design and drafting (CADD) and computer-aided manufacturing (CAM). These programs allow engineers to create complex 3-D drawings and manufacture parts on 3-D printers. Engineers also write computer code and create software to program robots.

Robotics engineers step away from their computers when working on prototype machines in a lab or setting up new robots on a factory floor. Engineer Tom Allen describes part of his day as a robotics research fellow working on autonomous mining vehicles:

> Perhaps we're testing a new path . . . algorithm [guiding a robot around] on the university lawn. Maybe I'm up on the electrical engineering tower installing a new GPS antenna. I could be lounging in a comfy couch reading some papers, or pacing around my office thinking through the consequences of a change to our [streaming] protocol.[24]

While robotics engineers might spend part of their day on their own, tech recruiter Lance Harvie writes: "Engineers have to function well in a team-oriented environment to accomplish tasks, especially when working on big projects."[25] In order to keep members of the vast team up-to-date on their work, robotics engineers often take part in what is called a daily standup, where they explain what they are working on. Robotics engineer Areeya Taylor, who works on an assistive robot named Misty, describes the daily standup:

> Each person quickly goes over what they did yesterday, what they're doing today, and whether they need any assistance. Today the Personality team is talking about how to make Misty's eyes be expressive according to the robot's current emotion. The Vision team is working on a new algorithm to get the robot to recognize its charger. The Programmability team is working on the new skill system. I'm working closely with the Core and Mobile teams on validating issues with network onboarding, so users can use the mobile app to put the robot onto the WIFI network reliably. [After the standup we] have an "after party" regarding outstanding issues with our current release.[26]

Education and Training

Anyone wishing to work designing and building robots needs at least a bachelor of science degree in mechanical, manufacturing, electrical, electronic, or industrial engineering. High school students who want a career designing, testing, and overseeing production of robotic equipment should focus on STEM subjects: science, technology, engineering, and math. Robotics engineers also make extensive use of physics and chemistry. Computer coding skills are very important in robotics. Engineers commonly work with C++, Python, and other programming languages. Beyond technical skills, robotics work relies on teamwork—communications classes like speech and writing help students learn to express their ideas more effectively.

College students working toward a bachelor's degree in engineering take courses that focus on pneumatics, hydraulics, CADD/CAM systems, logic, microprocessors, and integrated systems. Some robotics engineers work toward a bachelor's degree in one field, such as mechanical engineering, and a master's degree in another field like electronic engineering, qualifying them for upper-level positions in the industry.

Students in their sophomore year can apply for cooperative education programs (co-ops) at technology companies or at government research labs like the Jet Propulsion Laboratory in Pasadena, California. Students in co-ops stop taking classes to work full-time. The positions are typically paid and last anywhere from three to twelve months. Students receive an academic credit and letter grade for their paid work experience.

Robotics engineers who work at big companies or for the government are not required to have a special license. However, those who work for small businesses might need to become a certified PE. This requires the engineer to pass a Fundamentals of Engineering exam, work under a licensed PE for four years, and then take a Principles and Practice of Engineering exam.

Skills and Personality

Becoming a robotics engineer requires long hours of study of the most complex subjects imaginable. Successful engineers have ambition, analytical and scientific skills, and a passion for robotic technology. Engineers need to have excellent communication skills, technical knowledge, and the ability to plan and manage projects effectively and within budget.

In this ever-changing field, robotics engineers are committed to staying up-to-date on the latest developments in the field. This requires robotics engineers to be lifelong learners. They stay well informed by reading journals, websites, blogs, and research papers about the latest industry developments, progress in robotics, and efforts of others in the field. Robotics engineer Cagney Moreau says, "I spend a lot of time learning. It's much cheaper to watch someone else's mistake or learn how other people are succeeding or failing."[27]

Working Conditions

Robotics engineers might work by themselves in office settings, attend meetings, and work around robotic machinery on produc-

tion floors, which might require them to wear ear protection, goggles, and other safety equipment. Engineers in this field travel to conferences and factories where robotic machines are produced. Those with master's degrees might teach part-time or full-time.

Employers and Pay

Robotics engineers are employed in many fields today. Some robotics engineers conduct research and design robots for car companies like GM and Ford, while others work on autonomous automobiles for large technology companies such as Google and Apple. Engineers also work for major manufacturers of food and consumer goods, and some design assistive robots that perform a wide range of tasks. As the use of robots expands, robotics engineers will appear in many diverse industries.

The BLS does not provide a specific job listing for robotics engineer; the position is so new that there is not a lot of data to work with. The BLS categorizes robotics engineers with mechanical engineers, who earned an average median salary of $87,370 in 2018. The BLS does say that mechanical engineers

Bringing a Robot to Life

"In most cases your time is split between working at a computer, going to meetings (some productive, some aggravatingly time-wasting), testing code, PCBs [printed circuit boards], mechanisms in a lab; and the best part: working on and testing the robot itself. Given that there are usually not enough prototypes for testing/working on and that pieces often don't work as expected, the "robot testing" part does not happen as often as one would like. . . . I can say it has been consistently rewarding. It is always exciting to see a new robot come alive and start moving around on its own."

—Paul Sandin, robotics engineer

Paul Sandin, "What Does a Robotics Engineer's Day-to-Day Job Look Like?," Quora, April 28, 2017. www.quora.com.

who worked in scientific research and development—an area that would include robotics engineers—earned an annual average salary of $99,870. And as Frank Bertini, robotics business manager at Velodyne LiDAR, pointed out in 2019, there is a great demand for top-level robotics engineers: "People who can think, design, build, and program by themselves. . . . [Companies are offering] at least $250,000 to a master's or Ph.D.-level candidate with skills in machine vision, deep learning or machine learning."[28]

What Is the Future Outlook for Robotics Engineers?

The BLS predicts that the demand for all engineers will grow 5 percent through 2028, while projected job growth for mechanical engineers will be 4 percent. However, BLS statistics do not consider the fact that demand for robotics engineers in 2020 is outpacing supply. According to Andra Keay, managing director of Silicon Valley Robotics (SVR), "The problem is very serious. Competition is stiff for people who are useful in robotics. They often have the exact skills that are in high demand at every major technology company."[29] This means that the future outlook for robotics engineers is good and demand should be higher than predicted by the BLS.

Find Out More

International Federation of Robotics (IFR)

www.ifr.org

The IFR is an international organization that serves the robotics industry through publication of market data, white papers, and blogs, and by hosting symposia and other events. The IFR website provides prospective robotics engineers with learning tools concerning industrial robots, robotics research, and case studies.

Jet Propulsion Laboratory (JPL)

www.jpl.jobs

The Jet Propulsion Laboratory is a research and development center for robotic space and Earth science missions. The JPL website provides information about high-tech robotics jobs along with offers of internships and mentorships that would be of interest to prospective robotics engineers.

Robot Report

www.therobotreport.com

This website covers a wide range of subjects related to robotics engineering, technology, and business. Students interested in robotics can find current events, product information, and research along with webinars and downloadable reports that cover the development, integration, and use of robots.

Robotics Industry Association (RIA)

www.robotics.org

The RIA provides webinars, certifications, awards, and seminars to engineers, managers, and executives in the robotics industry. Students can find free educational resources such as a beginner's guide to robotics, technology papers, videos, and career advice on the RIA website.

Sales Engineer

What Does a Sales Engineer Do?

In 2019 dozens of start-up technology companies were competing to bring a new generation of advanced robotic equipment to businesses and consumers. While some of these companies had the technical know-how to create amazing robots, they struggled financially. Technology business journalist John K. Waters says that robotics equipment companies face challenges when it comes to finding new customers. "Sales and marketing aren't necessarily natural activities for engineers, but you can't build a robotics company from the lab," Waters observes. "Though it might seem obvious, this bit of wisdom is often ignored."[30] Some companies know there is a solution to this problem—they hire sales engineers. These professionals are trained engineers who focus on sales, marketing, and customer relations.

Sales engineers possess the extensive scientific and technical knowledge needed to sell complex services and equipment to businesses. Depending on where they work, they might be referred to as systems engineers, customer engineers, technical accounts managers, applications engineers, or field engineers. Some sales engineers

A Few Facts

Number of Jobs
66,700 in 2018

Pay
$101,429 average median wage in 2018

Educational Requirements
Bachelor of science degree in engineering

Personal Qualities
Good communicator, understands sales techniques, strong engineering skills

Work Settings
Offices, conference rooms, and factory floors

Future Job Outlook
6 percent growth through 2028

have the impressive-sounding title of chief evangelist. In this role, sales engineers act as fervent advocates for robotics technology. They try to persuade customers and the public that robots are indispensable tools that are having a positive effect on society.

Whatever the exact job title, sales engineers are team leaders with specialized business knowledge of concepts like project management, product development, and targeted marketing. They deliver technical demonstrations about complex equipment in a friendly and engaging manner to existing and prospective customers. Presentations might include informative slide shows, videos, and other marketing materials that can be easily understood by those with less technical training. Sales engineers also promote their products on social media. They write blogs, post photos of their company's robotic equipment on Instagram, provide product updates on Twitter, and post demonstration videos on YouTube. After a sale is made, sales engineers arrange delivery, consult with clients during installation, and follow up on orders to solve postsale problems.

Sales engineers at large companies might spend their time focusing on the technical aspects of the job while overseeing a team of sales representatives who concentrate on marketing and selling. These engineers might conduct product and marketing research while engaging with businesses to determine their technological needs. This research can be used by a sales engineer's employer to create new products or update existing ones.

A Typical Workday

Sales engineers are first and foremost salespeople. Many of their duties are similar to sales representatives in other industries. Sales engineers work in offices and conference rooms, where they lay out sales strategies in meetings with sales teams, business executives, and company planners. They share meals with potential clients in restaurants and travel to industry conferences and conventions to make sales presentations. Sales engineers show potential customers how equipment is used and how it will lower costs and increase production. These specialists help customers create specific solutions to their problems by presenting unique product configurations or demonstrating how equipment can be integrated into existing assembly lines. When closing a sale, sales engineers negotiate prices and sign contracts. Once a sale is completed, a sales engineer makes periodic follow-up calls to recommend new products to the client.

Sales engineers spend a portion of each day focusing on the engineering aspect of their job. They study the technical aspects of their products, read industry-related blogs, articles, and journals, and research the competition. And like most jobs, there is plenty of paperwork. Sales engineers fill out sales reports, draw up business proposals, and write reports about equipment problems.

Education and Training

Most sales engineers have a bachelor's degree in engineering or a related field such as computer science or mathematics. Most four-year college engineering programs require students to specialize in electronics, mechanical engineering, or other fields. However, not all sales engineers possess an engineering degree. Some began as sales representatives and, over time, developed a strong grasp of the technological aspects of their company's products.

High school students who hope to become sales engineers need to master complex subjects including algebra, calculus, probability, statistics, and algorithms. Students who excel in these subjects can learn independently by searching for machine learning tutorials and courses online. For example, some online universities offer machine learning "boot camp," courses that can be completed in two to four months, with one-on-one weekly mentor support. There are also numerous podcasts like DataHack Radio and Learning Machines 101 that provide insight into the profession.

College students who focus on robotics engineering take courses in computer science, AI, robotics, physics, and cognitive science. They study database theory, database design, and operating systems like Windows and Linux. Classes include storage technologies, networking, and database maintenance, recovery, and security.

Know Your Product

"Much of what I do . . . is helping explain how the platform works and walking users through the system. In doing so I am selling them on the intricacies of the platform that may not be readily apparent. What it really comes down to is being able to condense a lot of [confusing] techno-jargon into everyday English (or whatever other language your customers speak). It's a bit more than just being charismatic and selling someone on basic features using buzzwords. It demands a knowledge of the product that only comes with time."

—Joshua Melo, email automation system sales engineer

Joshua Melo, "What Does a Sales Engineer Do?," Quora, June 21, 2017. www.quora.com.

Those who wish to specialize in sales engineering might obtain a Master of Engineering Management (MEM) degree. This is a degree similar to Master of Business Administration (MBA) but with an emphasis on technology. Those who pursue MEM degrees complete courses in one to two years. The curriculum focuses on fundamentals of leadership, business law, and business administration. Graduates come away with the knowledge required to manage engineering projects and technology-based enterprises.

College students studying to become sales engineers can find plenty of internship programs that focus on robotics, engineering, and sales. Internships are available at robotics hardware manufacturers, technology start-ups, educational institutions, and government agencies. Career websites like LinkedIn and Glassdoor have numerous listings for summer internship positions for sales engineers in nearly every region of the country.

Few college graduates with engineering degrees will begin their careers as sales engineers. Most companies require engineers to train and gain sales experience before they can assume the position of sales engineer. Those in training might be required to attend company-specific sales and marketing seminars or be paired with a mentor. Prospective sales engineers will learn their employer's business practices and company culture. They will meet with established customers, sit in on sales presentations, and make sales calls to potential clients.

After trainees become sales engineers, they pursue self-education throughout their careers. The field of robotics is advancing so rapidly that the technical knowledge engineers gained in college can become obsolete in a few years. And sales engineers need to use their knowledge of the latest technological developments to make educated predictions about future trends.

Skills and Personality

Engineers are often painted as introverted, tech-loving nerds. But mechanical engineer Brandon R. Buckhalt works to dispel the stereotype: "Engineers are the builders, the believers, the inventors, the creative geniuses, and the optimistic go-getters."[31] Sales engineers who are go-getters believe in what they are selling. They support their company's mission and use their optimism to convince customers to buy its products.

Good sales engineers have strong character skills which help them establish rapport and trust. Workplace expert Amy Cooper Hakim asserts, "[Employers] look for those with excellent [character] skills to lead others, to gain customers and to share and promote ideas in group settings."[32] While character skills come naturally to some, others need to make an effort to perfect them. Job counselors say interactions with others are made easier by making eye contact. Looking into a person's eyes helps establish trust.

Anyone involved in sales needs to have excellent communication skills. Sales engineers are required to make clear and concise presentations that explain the details of highly technical processes in plain English. They also need to be confident and persuasive. Sales engineers need to express excitement in their product and convince clients to see how they would benefit by making a purchase. In addition to people skills, sales engineers need to have technical skills and an extensive understanding of the products they sell.

Working Conditions

Some sales engineers are assigned to territories which might cover several states. This requires them to travel extensively. These engineers work full-time, but the hours might include nights and weekends spent away from home. The job can be stressful since salespeople are often paid a base salary and a commission, which is a percentage of the purchase price of a product. While commissions can be high, months can pass between sales.

Employers and Pay

Sales engineers work for telecommunications companies, computer systems designers, electronics producers, and manufacturers. Those who specialize in robotics work in a rapidly changing field populated by innovative start-ups and established robotics makers like Mitsubishi and Rockwell Automation. Wherever they work, sales engineers can earn a good living collecting a salary, commissions, and bonuses. According to the BLS, sales engineers earned a median wage of $101,429 in 2018. The lowest 10 percent of sales engineers earned less than $58,430, while the highest 10 percent earned more than $165,350.

What Is the Future Outlook for Sales Engineers?

The BLS predicts employment for all sales engineers will grow 6 percent through 2028. However, the BLS also says that the demand for sales engineers in the general field of computer systems design and related services is projected to grow 24 percent through 2028. This job sector includes robotics equipment, which means the outlook for robotics sales engineers is very good.

Find Out More

Manufacturers' Agents National Association (MANA)
www.manaonline.org

MANA is a professional organization for sales representatives in the manufacturing industry. Its website features blogs and podcasts, and provides sales tips, marketing data, and other information of use to prospective sales engineers.

Manufacturers' Representatives Educational Research Foundation (MRERF)
www.mrerf.org

MRERF is an educational foundation aimed at sales representatives in the manufacturing industry. Prospective sales engineers can visit the website to learn about training and certification programs and other educational materials.

Robohub
www.robohub.org

Robohub is a communications platform used by experts in robotics start-ups, research, business, and education. The site features articles by robotics evangelists, sales engineers, and other professionals who share their knowledge and experiences in their own words.

Robotics Business Review
www.roboticsbusinessreview.com

This website focuses on the business aspects of robotics, providing information about sales and marketing robots in a number of industries. Prospective sales engineers can access the website for the latest news, research, webcasts, and information about educational institutions.

Data Scientist

A Few Facts

Number of Jobs
31,700

Pay
$108,000 median
annual salary in 2019

**Educational
Requirements**
Master's degree in
data science, computer
science, engineering,
mathematics

Personal Qualities
Highly developed
science and math skills,
business acumen, good
communicator, team
player

Work Settings
Full-time in offices

Future Job Outlook
16 percent growth
through 2028

What Does a Data Scientist Do?

In 2019 the job search website Glass-door named data scientist the best job in America for the fourth year in a row. According to Glassdoor, data scientists have high levels of job satisfaction and earn great salaries. And there are thousands of open jobs available for professionals in this field. These facts have driven an increasing number of college students to major in data science. While some of these students might be driven by the rosy job picture painted by Glassdoor, data science is not for everyone. Those who work in the profession have outstanding scientific, mathematical, and technical skills that can only be developed through hard work and experience.

The term *data* defines any set of facts collected for analysis. For example, a shopping website maintains a vast database filled with billions of pieces of data on its customers. These data include names, ages, phone numbers, addresses, credit card numbers, shopping histories, and even religious and political affiliations. How some or all of the data are used is up to the business

Understanding Data and Business

"When a business needs to answer a question or solve a problem, they turn to a data scientist to gather, process, and derive valuable insights from the data. Whenever data scientists are hired by an organization, they will explore all aspects of the business and develop programs using programming languages like Java to perform robust analytics. . . . Data scientists focus on the statistical analysis and research needed to determine which machine learning approach to use, then they model the algorithm and prototype it for testing."

—Andrew Zola, data scientist

Andrew Zola, "Machine Learning Engineer vs. Data Scientist," *Springboard Blog*, January 3, 2019. www.springboard.com.

and the expertise of data scientists. Data scientist Andrew Zola describes his profession and its function in business. "Data science can be described as the description, prediction, and causal inference from both structured and unstructured data," Zola writes. "This discipline helps individuals and enterprises make better business decisions."[33] In simpler terms, data scientists search for patterns in databases and analyze them to help companies make business decisions. In the case of an online retailer, a data scientist will study information concerning customer buying histories, product returns, economic cycles, seasonal purchases, and other factors. The retailer will use these data to time the release of new products, offer deals and sales specials, and hire and fire employees.

Looking at billions of pieces of data to provide solid business plans is tricky. But data scientists who work in the field of robotics must deal with problems that are even more complex. Driverless cars, which are basically robots with passenger seats, provide a good example of a data scientist's work. A self-driving machine relies on billions of bits of data provided by its global positioning system (GPS), video cameras, cloud-based maps, and numerous sensors that detect objects, lane markings, and the position of other vehicles.

Data scientists analyze and interpret all that data to "teach" the car to interact with the physical world. The scientists invent highly detailed software programs that help the car navigate through nearly every type of situation. Data scientist Fei Qi claims, "Data scientists are the pioneers behind perfecting the brain of the beast (driverless cars). We must somehow figure out how to develop algorithms that master Perception, Localization, Prediction, Planning, and Control."[34]

Perception helps the car "see," localization lets it know exactly where it is, prediction helps it identify potential hazards, and planning and control keep the car moving safely forward. Programming these processes into a robotic brain requires data scientists to use concepts of machine learning. In this process, the robot constantly collects data, interprets it, and updates its algorithms. According to Qi, "[Data scientists] take real-life driving experiences, turn them into programmable information, and train our models to continuously and self-sufficiently improve its understanding of the real world in order to make 'informed' decisions."[35]

A Typical Workday

Though an autonomous car might be driving on a test track or a highway, the data scientists plotting its path spend very little time outdoors. The job requires them to spend long hours at their desks performing statistical analysis on computers. According to a 2016 survey of data scientists by *Forbes*, these professionals spend 60 percent of their time organizing data and cleaning data (detecting, correcting, and deleting inaccurate or irrelevant portions of data). Collecting data takes up about 20 percent of a data scientist's time. This means data scientists spend 80 percent of their time preparing and managing data for analysis. And according to *Forbes*, eight out of ten data scientists consider these tasks to be the least enjoyable part of their job.

Once the data are cleaned and standardized for practical use, data scientists mine the data in search of patterns to analyze. During this process, they refine algorithms and build training sets for machine learning. Describing the job, technology journalist Mary Shacklett writes, "Data science can require extended periods of concentration. This work is best done alone and with minimal interruption. If you are a highly social person and desire constant interaction, a data science career might be too isolating."[36] On the bright side, data scientists can work wherever they have the computing power to perform their jobs. Some avoid commutes and other hassles by working from home.

Education and Training

Most data scientists have a master's degree in data science, computer science, engineering, mathematics, or related fields. According to a data scientist known by the pseudonym Simplilearn,

> Data scientists are highly educated—88 percent have at least a master's degree and 46 percent have PhDs—and while there are notable exceptions, a very strong educational background is usually required to develop the depth of knowledge necessary to be a data scientist.[37]

Students who hope to become data scientists should be able to understand programming languages like Python, R, and SQL. Many colleges and universities offer data science boot camp— four- to six-month crash courses in coding, machine learning, data science, and other relevant topics. Students should also take as many math courses as they can and study database theory, database design, and operating systems like Windows and Linux.

After high school, prospective data scientists will earn a bachelor's degree in data science, statistics, physics, applied business analytics, bioinformatics, or related subjects. These courses teach students basics like experimentation, quantitative problem solving, and handling data sets. Those who wish to go into the robotics industry might seek an advanced degree in computer science, engineering, physics, or mathematics.

Skills and Personality

Data scientists are highly organized people with skills in mathematics and analytics. They have strong powers of concentration, an eye for detail, and the ability to work alone with mind-boggling

Try, Try Again

"Data science is experimental work. You're trying different algorithms against different combinations of data. Like most researchers, data scientists encounter many failures because not every algorithm or theory works. Great data scientists know when to quit and when to try another approach. When they fail, they try again. . . . Sometimes unique insights can turn up from nowhere. In other cases, what you think was a good formula or algorithm to apply to the data yields nothing. A data scientist job is not for someone who likes coming to work each morning already understanding how their day is going to go."

—Mary Shacklett, technology journalist

Mary Shacklett, "10 Signs You May Not Be Cut Out for a Data Scientist Job," TechRepublic, October 9, 2018. www.techrepublic.com.

piles of data day after day. Data scientists are extremely competent coders who work with one or more programming languages.

In addition to technical and scientific talents, data scientists need business acumen. As Simplilearn explains, "To be a data scientist you'll need a solid understanding of the industry you're working in, and know what business problems your company is trying to solve. . . . You need to know about how businesses operate so you can direct your efforts in the right direction."[38]

In addition to understanding how a company operates, data scientists need to work efficiently in a business environment. They participate in company meetings where they are required to explain their complex data analyses to engineers, marketers, operations managers, CEOs, and others. As data scientist Adam Kovarik writes, data scientists have to communicate clearly and in plain English; they do not need to expound on their esoteric research points. He maintains:

[Coworkers] have decisions to make and a bottom line to impact. You are in that room giving that presentation for one simple reason: to improve the business. . . . Those people [in the meeting] want the tools and information at their fingertips to make the business better. Focusing on the minutia may sell your intellect, but it may also disconnect you from the true goals of the organization. Once this happens, your analysis becomes a footnote.[39]

Kovarik also says that listening is as important as talking. He says data scientists should listen closely to others as they talk and always take notes at meetings: "Establish a note-taking system early and consistently. Use OneNote, Evernote, Notepad, paper and pencil. . . . It does not matter. Your future self will thank you."[40]

Working Conditions

Data scientists work in offices, oftentimes solving complex problems with little input from others. They also attend meetings to work on strategies with company executives, develop new products with engineers, and create advertising campaigns with marketers.

Employers and Pay

Nearly every company relies on technology to maximize profits. Businesses make important decisions based on information gleaned from digital sources. Data scientists are the people who make sense of this information, and they work in almost every business sector.

Data scientists are employed by major online retailers such as Amazon; they work for social media companies including Facebook and Instagram; and they analyze data for banks, insurance companies, and the health care industry. Those who specialize in robotics are employed by automotive and technology companies working to perfect self-driving cars, such as Apple, Google, Tesla, and General Motors. Wherever data scientists work, they can expect to earn six-figure salaries. According to Glassdoor, the median salary for data scientists was $108,000 in 2019.

What Is the Future Outlook for Data Scientists?

The BLS says the demand for data scientists is expected to grow by 16 percent through 2028, much faster than the average for all occupations. Glassdoor analyst Allison Berry explains, "One of the big reasons we continue to see such demand for data scientists is every company out there is becoming a tech company. In any industry that has to deal with digitized data, or has an app or an online presence, you need people who can help support all of that and find insights from the data."[41]

Find Out More

American Physical Society (APS)
www.aps.org

The APS works to advance science, science education, and the science community. The organization supports physics educators and students at all levels through its programs, publications, and resources.

Association for Computing Machinery (ACM)
www.acm.org

ACM is a professional organization for data scientists, computing educators, and researchers. The association has over eight hundred local chapters worldwide open to students and professionals. The ACM website offers educational resources for students including technology talks, journals, and research papers.

National Center for Women and Information Technology (NCWIT)
www.ncwit.org

This organization works to increase the participation of girls and women in computer science fields. NCWIT is focused on students and offers a wide range of educational resources, including videos, blogs, and a newsletter.

TDWI Upside
https://tdwi.org/pages/upside.aspx

This website is aimed at data scientists and prospective data scientists. TDWI provides workshops and onsite courses on data modeling, business analytics, advanced data science, and leadership and management. Research resources include webinars, e-books, reports, and infographics.

Mathematician

What Does a Mathematician Do?

In 2017 Google Doodle commemorated a device that it said "opened up a skyful of knowledge and inspiration."[42] The robotic mechanism was created to predict the positions of the planets and stars and the timing of eclipses decades in advance. The robot, with the tongue twisting name "Antikythera mechanism," used advanced mathematical theories to make incredibly accurate predictions. And this complex melding of mathematics and machinery was made over 2,100 years ago by unknown Greek inventors who possessed an extensive knowledge of algebra, geometry, calculus, and other mathematical concepts. The existence of the Antikythera mechanism proves that math and robotics have been intertwined for as long as humans have dreamed of producing self-operating machines. As mathematics professor Florian Potra writes, "The idea of a robot may be as old as the earliest mathematical studies."[43]

While today's robots are far more complex than those invented in the first century BC, autonomous machines like self-driving cars and assistive robots would still not exist without mathematicians. These professionals work with numbers and their applications in geometry, algebra, computational mathematics, applied mathematics, and other types of math to solve problems in economics, engineering, business, physics, medicine, and other sciences. Mathematicians conduct research and experiment with existing mathematical principles to discover new principles. The job is extremely complex, as math student Apurv Narayan makes clear:

> Specific duties might include . . . analyzing data and developing algorithms, computational methods and statistical models to reveal relationships between the data elements. You could also design or decipher encryptions systems for military, law enforcement, governmental or business applications. As a scholar, you'll also spend time reading mathematical journals and participating in conferences to stay abreast of developments in the field.[44]

Mathematicians who specialize in robotics conduct research concerning movements of robotic arms and legs, and write software to control the movements of the machines. This requires a background in computational number theory, modular arithmetic, calculus, linear algebra, graph theory, and probability. Robotics mathematicians also rely on the knowledge of obscure concepts like Bayesian inference (a technique of statistics) and kinematics, which focuses on the position, velocity, and acceleration of objects and groups of objects. Mathematics professor Syed Zain Mahdi states, "[Robotics is] all mathematics. It's the foundation that allows us to analyze and define definite rules aiding our aims for robotic design and development. . . . We utilize mathematical formulations from different fields . . . to formulate new and innovative concepts."[45]

A Typical Workday

Mathematicians who work in robotics spend their days conceiving of AI algorithms and analyzing software programs. They might have hands-on interaction with robotic machinery, conducting integration tests to ensure software works properly with physical hardware. When searching for answers, mathematicians might

Sought-After Math Pros

"Mathematicians are able to read articles in almost any scientific or technical field. They are sought after for the more difficult software jobs such as writing and improving CG effects used for films. . . . Machine vision, including defect analysis, pattern recognition and automatic alignment, is math-intensive. Audio processing and design of music synthesizers is pure, sometimes heavy, math. . . . [My] degree in applied math has enabled me to switch careers whenever I felt like a change. I have designed software systems, robotics, ultrasonic transducers, microscopes (including custom lens design and digital holography), analog circuits, and digital automotive circuits."

—David W. Vogel, engineer

David W. Vogel, "Are Math Majors Jobless?," Quora, January 15, 2018. www.quora.com.

use GitHub, an online collaboration tool that allows them to consult with others working in robotics, AI, and machine learning.

Most mathematicians work full-time. But it is commonly said that mathematicians can only work for three hours at a time before the mental gymnastics of the job require them to rest. Perhaps this is why tech companies and other employers often allow mathematicians to set their own schedules and even work from home. In 2016 mathematician Alec Wilson described his workweek:

> Last Friday I got to the office at 10am, worked for 3 hours until about 1pm and then left. That entire time was spent working solidly on mathematics. Today, I worked from home from 9am to 11am then went to the office and worked there from about 12pm to 4pm and then came back home and have continued working since I got back.[46]

Education and Training

Some mathematicians have only a bachelor's degree in mathematics, which qualifies them to work for federal government agencies. However, most employers who hire mathematicians require advanced degrees, either a master of science in mathematics or a doctorate in math.

High school students who hope to become mathematicians need to take as many math courses as possible, including geometry, algebra, statistics, and calculus. Since most math professionals also create data analysis software, students should become proficient coders familiar with programming languages such as Arduino IDE, Python, and C or C+.

Prospective mathematicians should consider attending summer enrichment programs in math, commonly referred to as math summer camps. These programs are more fun than sitting in algebra class. Campers create apps, work on puzzles, participate in competitions, meet professionals in the field, and even build robots. Summer enrichment programs are often hosted by colleges and universities and can be found in most states. The American Mathematical Society website features a detailed list of residential programs nationwide. In addition to boosting their learning, those who participate in math summer camps show that they are motivated students who have an interest in academics. This can enhance college applications.

College students studying for a bachelor's degree in mathematics take advanced math courses, such as differential equations and linear and abstract algebra. Most educational institutions require students to take related courses in computer science, engineering, or physics. Postgraduate students obtain degrees in theoretical or applied mathematics. Those who wish to go into robotics focus on applied mathematics, which is concerned with solving practical problems. (Theoretical mathematics is focused on math theory and less concerned with practical applications.)

Math master's programs involve courses in real analysis, complex analysis, probability, scientific computing, and differential equations. Students learn through a combination of lectures and seminars and also spend time working independently to solve problems. Those who pursue a doctoral degree in mathematics immerse themselves in extremely complex subjects, including the theory of mathematics, mathematical logic, statistical and mathematical analysis, topology, and stochastic processes.

Skills and Personality

While math can be mind-bogglingly complex, at its most basic it is about solving puzzles, and most mathematicians love tackling problems. Mathematicians spend their days with robotics engineers and scientists reviewing problems and seeking out new solutions. As mathematician Joseph Wong writes, "Good mathematicians are the ones who believe there is a solution to every problem and they can find a way to show you with numbers."[47]

Mathematicians obviously love math. Some even see magnificence in math formulas that can equal the aesthetic splendor of a symphony or painting. Physicist Clara Moskowitz says, "Mathematical equations aren't just useful—many are quite beautiful. And many [mathematicians] admit they are often fond of particular formulas not just for their function, but for their form, and the simple, poetic truths they contain."[48]

Beyond the ability to find poetic truth in math, mathematicians need extremely strong analytical skills. When working to perfect robotic AI and machine learning programs, math professionals comb through massive amounts of data. They need to remember the smallest details in order to form analytical opinions. This task requires mathematicians to perfect their coding skills as they often write customized software programs to develop new techniques and models.

Like most high-tech workers, mathematicians need to be able to explain their work to associates including engineers, scientists, business and marketing managers, and others who are less proficient in math. This requires excellent communication skills. Mathematics professor John Baez writes, "Explaining things is a great way to clarify one's ideas, especially if you demand of yourself that your explanations be as clear as possible, with as little jargon as possible."[49]

Working Conditions

Mathematicians perform a variety of tasks while working in offices, research centers, and classrooms. Mathematician Colleen Farrelly says she spends a lot of her time "reading other people's papers and working on projects for my employer related to research & development, [applying] algorithms/research on real-

Some mathematicians can only work for a few hours at a time before the mental stress of the job requires them to rest. Some employers allow mathematicians to set their own schedules or work from home.

world data or simulations, writing up results/presenting results to non-mathematicians (mainly scientists and business folks), and introducing lay audiences to topics in mathematics."[50]

Mathematicians who work in robotics are team players who are in constant consultation with engineers, researchers, physicists, and other highly educated people. In this competitive environment, things do not always go smoothly. And it helps to have a sense of humor as demonstrated by mathematician Robert Gillespie's description of his typical workday in robotics research:

> First you wake up and get yelled at by the engineers. Then the operations research people call you and yell about the engineers. Then the systems analysts call up to yell about the operations research people. The physicists call you to tell you that your differential equations are wrong. . . . The theoretical computer scientists call you to prove to you that the systems analysts are wrong. Then the systems analysts write a computer program to prove the theoretical computer scientists wrong, and they just sit there arguing endlessly. While you slip out quietly . . . and wish you were doing computer game programming.[51]

Math at Home and the Office

"I've heard it said that it's not possible to do more than 3 hours [of] useful mathematics in a day. Now, that clearly depends on the individual and is really about what you can consistently do—I've no doubt many mathematicians have days when they are more productive than that. The same adage probably applies to other creative work too. . . . Most mathematicians, in my experience, work full office hours and also take their work home with them."

—Stephen Miller, mathematician

Stephen Miller, "How Long Do Mathematicians Work in One Day?," Quora, November 19, 2016. www.quora.com.

Employers and Pay

Mathematicians work for banks as asset management researchers. They are employed by insurance companies and government agencies to provide statistical analysis. Some math professionals work in high-end research centers like the CERN particle physics laboratory in Switzerland or JPL in Pasadena. Mathematicians employed by robot makers develop algorithms and optimization formulas used in software.

The salaries paid to mathematicians vary according to industry. The BLS says the average median salary for a mathematician was $101,900 in 2018. However, those who worked in research and development for engineering firms earned $110,510, while technical consultants were averaging $116,210 annually. On the other end of the pay scale, mathematicians who work for colleges and universities earn an average salary of $61,440.

What Is the Future Outlook for Mathematicians?

Mathematicians are in high demand across a wide range of industries including robotics, AI, and machine learning. According to the BLS, employment for mathematicians is expected to grow by 30 percent through 2028. The largest demand for math professionals will come from the communications and medical manufacturing industries.

Find Out More

American Mathematical Society (AMS)

www.ams.org

The AMS represents mathematicians, researchers, and educators. It promotes mathematics research through the publication of books, journals, and blogs, and sponsors programs for student education. The society's website lists information about math summer camps in nearly every state.

Mathematical Association of America (MAA)

www.maa.org

The MAA is an international community of mathematicians, computer scientists, STEM professionals, students, and teachers. The association hosts competitions, provides curriculum resources, and offers student resources, including problem-solving books and information about regional conferences.

Robotics Education Competition Foundation (REC)

www.roboticseducation.org

The REC was founded to increase student interest in science, technology, engineering, and math. The foundation provides programs, workshops, and contests focused on robotics and other technology and sponsors Girl Powered, a program designed to mentor female students.

Society for Industrial and Applied Mathematics (SIAM)

www.siam.org

This professional society caters to mathematicians and researchers in business, government, and science. SIAM provides students access to videos, handbooks, competitions, and information about summer schools, internships, and careers in math.

Computer and Information Research Scientist

What Does a Computer and Information Research Scientist Do?

News articles about artificial intelligence appear on a daily basis. Artificial intelligence, also referred to as AI and machine learning, allows robots to teach themselves to make decisions without human input. AI is being put to use to drive autonomous cars, ferret out fake news on social media, catch cybercriminals, and even guide killer drones on the battlefield. The scientists behind these advances are known as computer and information research scientists. Depending on their jobs, they might also be referred to as AI scientists or information technology (IT) scientists. Whatever the job title, these research scientists are members of the fastest-growing job sector in the United States.

Computer and information research scientists are prominent in businesses that specialize in computers and robotics. They are also found in the aerospace, transportation, and communications industries. The scientists conduct in-depth research to help engineers design games and gaming hardware, navigation and guidance systems, telephones, cars, and other widely used products. AI scientists who work in the entertainment industry are responsible for the AI programs that suggest music and movies to users of Netflix, Spotify, and other streaming services.

Anyone who uses Google Search, Maps, or Google Now interacts with the work of AI scientists. These professionals perfect Google's ability to mine data, translate languages, analyze hardware and software performance, address customer complaints, prevent fraud, and improve core search functions. And Google AI research scientists are also pursuing next-generation robotic systems on a project known as DeepMind. The brain that powers DeepMind utilizes a network of circuits, called a neural network, that functions like a human brain. DeepMind intern Ji-Sung Kim describes the basic work performed by the project scientists: "You work on applied or fundamental research projects which push the boundaries of knowledge. You tend to publish papers and build software systems in collaboration with software/research engineers."[52]

In 2019 DeepMind made headlines when it beat two top-ranked video game professionals five times in a row while playing *StarCraft II*. Eventually the computer and information research scientists working on DeepMind plan to teach it the skills necessary to run online retail operations.

A Typical Workday

Anyone employed as a researcher is compelled to read—and read some more. As AI researcher Richard Waltman writes, on an average day he might

> read manuals for hardware (new and old), read language references to learn the inner workings of all available programming languages that are capable of self-editing . . . read dissertations and academic papers on topology, set theory, logic, complexity, and information theory . . . [and] read and meditate on philosophy/math/physics/logic (often in German, Latin, Greek, etc.).[53]

Waltman says he also spends time as an AI evangelist. In this role, he writes blogs and articles aimed at teaching the public about machine learning and the benefits of AI.

Some of the most important work performed by computer and information research scientists involves writing, testing, and analyzing complex machine learning algorithms. AI consultant Raman Deep S. Arora explains, "Machine Learning algorithms [are] the point where real AI starts. Using these algorithms you can improvise your output each time by making your model to remember its mistakes and not repeat them."[54]

As Waltman makes clear, working on high-level technical research requires scientists to meditate (concentrate their thoughts) on various subjects. On one level, they think about big-picture ideas: how they can improve a customer or business user's experience. On the other hand, AI research scientists meditate on real-world applications. They think of ways they can tweak software or solve a specific technical problem. AI researcher John Sanders describes how he approaches this aspect of his job:

> The key to research is to ask yourself a question which won't go away—often it happens by accident. Usually there is an answer somewhere and over a time, if you keep looking, you will find that [answer]. It only takes one question that is unanswered to cause you to become obsessive—then research becomes a compulsion.[55]

In addition to deep thinking, computer and information research scientists function as team leaders in the workplace. They schedule and attend meetings, hire and fire employees, evaluate project performance data, and create proposals for new projects. Researchers are responsible for explaining their projects, project goals, and policies to coworkers and management. They might also participate in multidisciplinary projects with outside sources at universities or research labs.

Find Out What Your Peers Are Doing

"At an abstract level, research, AI or otherwise, is about reading the literature in the field to understand what your peers are exploring and discovering. You pay particular attention to the sections of the papers where the authors describe what remains to be done or explored. After pulling together enough open issues, you identify an area where you can advance the thinking or understanding. Then you set off to prove your hypothesis using the appropriate scientific methods."

—Jay Swartz, artificial intelligence researcher

Jay Swartz, "What Is It Like to Do AI Research?," Quora, August 2, 2014. www.quora.com.

Education and Training

Computer and information research scientists typically have degrees in computer engineering, software engineering, information systems, IT, or a related field. While a bachelor's degree might be adequate for entry-level jobs in the field, most employers require information research scientists to have a master's degree. Those who wish to conduct pure research need a PhD.

Becoming a computer and information research scientist is a long-term goal that requires education, experience, and determination. High school students who hope to work as computer and information research scientists should focus on math courses including calculus, statistics, trigonometry, and algebra. Students should take physics, chemistry, and communications as well as computer science classes. Coding is central to a career as a computer and information research scientist, and students can learn important programming languages like R, Python, and SQL online. Working on hobby projects can also be beneficial to students.

Those pursuing a bachelor's degree take courses in programming, software development, math, and coding. Students study linear algebra, optimization, neuroscience, cognitive science, algorithms, and the theory of computation. Internships provide an opportunity to observe professional computer and information research scientists at work. Interns gain valuable experience man-

Computer and information research scientists frequently work in teams. Some of their most important work involves writing, testing, and analyzing complex machine learning algorithms.

aging and troubleshooting problems with computers, software, robotics equipment, and other technology. While working as interns, students can expand their networks, gaining contacts with those who can provide references and job recommendations after graduation.

Skills and Personality

Software developer Hernan Santiesteban says, "Computer and information research scientists need a wide variety of skills to be successful. Aside from the obvious importance of technical knowledge, oftentimes softer skills can play a more essential role."[56] Technical knowledge includes a good understanding of circuit boards, processors, chips, computer hardware and software, and other electronics. Scientists in this field rely on analytical skills to troubleshoot software and equipment and find innovative ways to solve problems. They use logic and reasoning to identify the strengths and weaknesses of the solutions they come up with to fix problems.

Softer skills are needed for computer and information research scientists who are often team leaders. These scientists work with systems analysts, engineers, project managers, department heads, managers, and vendors. They need to listen to coworkers and clearly present information and ideas to others.

Computer and information research scientists require business acumen. They understand that conducting research is extremely expensive. In this environment, computer and information research scientists are required to understand the economic principles and other business concepts driving their research. Employers need to make a profit on their research investments at some point in the future. For example, Google spends millions of dollars on self-driving car research, money it expects to recoup in five or ten years when its robotic systems are sold to car companies and taxi services.

Working Conditions

Most computer and information research scientists work forty hours per week in offices, laboratories, and in workshops. When major projects are nearing completion and deadlines are looming, they might work overtime, including nights and weekends. With the computer, software, and robotics industries changing very rapidly, computer and information research scientists regularly toil to update their knowledge and skills. They take online courses and might even attend college classes. And as computer science professor Ahmed Abdel-Fattah explains, seminars can provide a rich learning environment:

> You need to actively participate in conferences, meet and socialize with experts in the field, and make good connections (this is important!). Conferences (even the unknown ones held nowhere famous) may be a very good start, because you'll meet several 'minds' that you can discuss (or adopt) ideas with (or from, respectively).[57]

Employers and Pay

Around 25 percent of computer and information research scientists work for the federal government in Washington, DC. They might work in cybersecurity, developing AI programs to detect hacks and computer viruses. Others hold top-secret clearances at the Department of Defense, where they develop drones and other robotic weapons systems. Computer and information research scientists in the technology industry work at engineering firms and in research and development departments of corporations like Apple and Google. The greatest concentration of these robotics professionals can be found in technology hubs like San Francisco and the Silicon Valley in California, and in Seattle and New York City.

The median annual salary for computer and information research scientists in 2019 was $118,370. Those who were employed in the software industry earned the highest wage, around $140,000. Research scientists who were employed in the robotics industry earned an average salary of $128,570.

What Is the Future Outlook for Computer and Information Research Scientists?

The work of computer and information research scientists helps turn cutting-edge ideas into reality for businesses that produce robotics, software, computers, and a host of other items. According to the BLS, these specialists are in high demand; employment for computer and information research scientists is expected to grow by 16 percent through 2028.

Find Out More

Association for the Advancement of Artificial Intelligence (AAAI)
https://aaai.org

The AAAI is a scientific society focused on pairing thought and intelligent behavior with computers. AI is spreading into IT applications, and the AAAI offers conferences, workshops, periodicals, and books for prospective IT managers. The society also provides student scholarships, grants, and other honors.

Computing Research Association (CRA)
https://cra.org

The CRA is dedicated to linking computer researchers from industry, academia, and government. The association has a strong focus on students, and its website provides information about research grants, awards programs, graduate school options, and career building.

IEEE Computer Society
www.computer.org

The IEEE Computer Society is dedicated to computer science and technology and provides information about networking and career development for educators, scientists, engineers, and students. The website contains numerous educational and career-building resources, including online webinars and certification preparation.

USENIX Association
www.usenix.org

USENIX is also known as the Advanced Computing Systems Association. It is a community of engineers, scientists, and technicians that promotes research and shares information. The USENIX student section provides technology sessions and tutorials, grants, and information about student paper awards.

Source Notes

The Robot Revolution

1. Quoted in Yahoo! Finance, "Six Smart Factory Developments Likely in 2020," September 24, 2019. https://finance.yahoo.com.

Electromechanical Engineer

2. Quoted in Christopher Quinn, "Machines Drive Textile Industry Comeback Bid in South," *Atlanta Journal-Constitution*, March 21, 2019. www.ajc.com.
3. Quoted in Elka Torpey, "Robotics Technician," Bureau of Labor Statistics, October 2018. www.bls.gov.
4. Quoted in Karen Triano Golin, "A Maintenance Technician Right Out of High School," Lancaster Online, September 30, 2019. https://lancasteronline.com.
5. Quoted in *Modern Materials Handling*, "MRO Spotlight: Kara Powers, Darana Hybrid," August 24, 2017. www.mmh.com.
6. Quoted in *Modern Materials Handling*, "Technician Spotlight: Brian Lentz, Swisslog," March 1, 2015. www.mmh.com.
7. Quoted in *Modern Materials Handling*, "Technician Spotlight: Kenneth Mainville, SSI Schaefer Systems International," June 18, 2019. www.mmh.com.
8. Quoted in Dave Perkon, "Do Machines Dream?," Control Design, 2019. www.controldesign.com.
9. Quoted in Perkon, "Do Machines Dream?"

Robotics Programmer

10. Quoted in Ben Linders, "Q&A on the Book *The Driver in the Driverless Car*," InfoQ, September 21, 2019. www.infoq.com.
11. Brian Feldman, "What Programming Skills Are Required for a Robotics Engineer?," Quora, November 18, 2014. www.quora.com.

12. Quoted in Chris Stewart, "Interview: A Day in the Life of a Programmer," JaxEnter, September 6, 2019. https://jaxenter .com.
13. Alex Owen-Hill, "How to Be a Great Robot Programmer," *RobotIQ*, April 6, 2016. https://blog.robotiq.com.
14. Quoted in Hope Reese, "The Next Big Job in Tech: Robot Programmer," TechRepublic, November 28, 2016. www .techrepublic.com.

Manufacturing Engineer

15. Andy Orin, "Career Spotlight: What I Do as a Manufacturing Engineer," Lifehacker, September 18, 2015. https://lifehack er.com.
16. Quoted in Mars International, "A Day in the Life of a Manufacturing Engineer," November 23, 2016. www.marsint.com.
17. Orin, "Career Spotlight."
18. Joe Dyer, "A Day in the Life of a Manufacturing Engineer," DISHER, August 17, 2017. https://disher.com.
19. Elizabeth Walker, "A Day in the Life of Manufacturing Engineer Elizabeth Walker," All Together, March 11, 2019. https://all together.swe.org.
20. Dyer, "Day in the Life."
21. Quoted in Mars International, "Day in the Life."
22. Walker, "Day in the Life."

Robotics Engineer

23. Quoted in Irish Central, "Trinity College Socially Assistive Robot 'Stevie II' a Big Hit with US Vets," May 15, 2019. www .irishcentral.com.
24. Tom Allen, "What Does a Robotics Engineer's Day-to-Day Job Look Like?," Quora, April 13, 2019. www.quora.com.
25. Lance Harvie, "Five Ways to Improve Engineering Teams," Medium, October 9, 2018. https://medium.com.
26. Areeya Taylor, "A Day in the Life of a Robot Test Engineer," Misty Robotics, June 12, 2018. www.mistyrobotics.com.

27. Cagney Moreau, "What Does a Robotics Engineer's Day-to-Day Job Look Like?," Quora, April 13, 2019. www.quora.com.
28. Quoted in Eugene Demaitre, "Robots.Jobs Addresses Robotics Skills Shortage With a National Approach," The Robot Report, February 6, 2019. www.therobotreport.com.
29. Quoted in Demaitre, "Robots.Jobs."

Sales Engineer

30. John K. Waters, "Top 6 Business Takeaways from RoboBusiness 2019," Robotics Business Review, October 8, 2019. www.roboticsbusinessreview.com.
31. Brandon R. Buckhalt, "About," Creative Engineer, 2018. www.thecreativeengineer.com.
32. Quoted in Lindsay Tigar, "7 Indispensable Soft Skills to Develop for 2018," Ladders, December 12, 2017. www.theladders.com.

Data Scientist

33. Andrew Zola, "Machine Learning Engineer vs. Data Scientist," *Springboard Blog*, January 3, 2019. www.springboard.com.
34. Fei Qi, "The Data Science Behind Self-Driving Cars," Medium, April 22, 2019. https://medium.com.
35. Qi, "Data Science."
36. Mary Shacklett, "10 Signs You May Not Be Cut Out for a Data Scientist Job," TechRepublic, October 9, 2018. www.techrepublic.com.
37. Simplilearn, "9 Must-Have Skills You Need to Become a Data Scientist, Updated," KDnuggets, May 2018. www.kdnuggets.com.
38. Simplilearn, "9 Must-Have Skills."
39. Adam Kovarik, "Beyond the Technical: Connecting Data Skills to Business Skills," StatTrak, July 1, 2019. https://stattrak.amstat.org.
40. Kovarik, "Beyond the Technical."
41. Quoted in Alison DeNisco Rayome, "How to Become a Data Scientist: A Cheat Sheet," TechRepublic, May 3, 2019. www.techrepublic.com.

Mathematician

42. Quoted in Chiara Palazzo, "What is the Antikythera Mechanism? How Was this Ancient 'Computer' Discovered?," *Telegraph*, May 17, 2017. www.telegraph.co.uk.
43. Quoted in Mathematical Association of America, "Mathematics and Robotics," 2019. www.maa.org.
44. Apurv Narayan, "Does a Bachelor's Degree in Mathematics Qualify One to be Called a Mathematician?," Quora, December 31, 2015. www.quora.com.
45. Syed Zain Mahdi, "What Are the Math Prerequisites for Robotics?," Quora, January 24, 2018. www.quora.com.
46. Alec Wilson, "How Long Do Mathematicians Work in One Day?," Quora, November 21, 2016. www.quora.com.
47. Joseph Wong, "What Makes Someone a Good Mathematician?," Quora, January 28, 2016. www.quora.com.
48. Clara Moskowitz, "The 11 Most Beautiful Mathematical Equations," Live Science, June 1, 2017. www.livescience.com.
49. John Baez, "What's a Day Like in the Life of a Mathematician?," Quora, July 23, 2015. www.quora.com.
50. Colleen Farrelly, "What's a Day Like in the Life of a Mathematician?," Quora, March 26, 2018. www.quora.com.
51. Robert Gillespie, "What is Your Work Day Like as an Applied Mathematician?," Quora, February 19, 2017. www.quora.com.

Computer and Information Research Scientist

52. Ji-Sung Kim, "What Is It Like to Be an AI Scientist Working at DeepMind?," Quora, September 4, 2018. www.quora.com.
53. Richard Waltman, "What Does an AI Research Engineer Work Day Look Like?," Quora, September 4, 2018. www.quora.com.
54. Raman Deep S. Arora, "Where Do I Start A Career Path in AI?," Quora, May 6, 2017. www.quora.com.
55. John Sanders, "What Is It Like to Do AI Research?," Quora, July 14, 2018. www.quora.com.
56. Quoted in Moira Alexander, "Why Emotional Intelligence is Key for Project Success," TechRepublic, May 5, 2017. www.techrepublic.com.
57. Ahmed Abdel-Fattah, "How Can I Become an AI Scientist?," Quora, September 7, 2018. www.quora.com.

Interview with a Robotics Engineer

Rich Hooper is a robotics engineer. As principal systems engineer, he has worked on multimillion-dollar projects for the US Air Force and US Army. He has several engineering degrees and a PhD in robotics. Hooper answered the following interview questions by email.

Q: What is a principal engineer?
A: This title is typically reserved for the highest-level group of engineers in an organization. Principal Engineers provide guidance to multiple teams of engineers working on different projects.

Q: Why did you become a robotics engineer?
A: I'm not sure why I became a robotics engineer, but here's how it happened. In one of my high-school science classes we learned about the Watt governor. The Watt governor is a type of feedback controller that ran early steam engines. This led me to servos (small motors that add movement to robotic mechanisms), which led me to decide to build a robotic hand as a teenager in my parent's garage. I barely got the servo part working, but it was a start.

Later I went to college to get an undergraduate degree as an electrical engineer. After that I worked as an electrical engineer for a few years. During this time, I designed several automatic control systems that were very interesting. One of them controlled a motor with an armature as big as a phone booth! Then I went back to school, this time as a mechanical engineer, and completed the undergraduate mechanical engineering curriculum. After that it was a master's degree in biomedical engineering and the PhD where I focused on robotics.

Q: Do you have any certifications?

A: I am a Professional Engineer, which is often abbreviated as "PE" and not to be confused with a Principal Engineer. A Professional Engineer is a person who by reason of their knowledge of mathematics, the physical sciences and the principles of engineering, acquired by professional education and practical experience, is qualified to engage in the practice of professional engineering. To lawfully use that title a person must pass a series of exams, have multiple years of engineering experience, at least five positive references from other professional engineers and maintain a license from the state in which they practice. A Professional Engineer is licensed by one or more states (I am registered in Texas) to practice engineering in matters of public safety. Consequently, the requirements for becoming a PE are quite stringent.

Q: What is your typical workday like?

A: I generally get to work at 8:00 AM. Then I'll:

- Spend two or three hours designing electrical circuits or mechanical systems and helping younger engineers learn about these circuits and systems. These engineers also help me by creating drawings and schematics.
- Spend an hour or two working on bills of materials (BOMs); the BOM is very important to engineers. This is a list of all the materials in the system. It includes wires, resistors, integrated circuits, nuts, bolts and processors, etc. The manufacturing department uses the BOMs and the drawings to build the systems.
- An hour or two in meetings or conference calls.
- An hour or two writing emails.
- An hour or two in the lab conducting experiments or trying to understand why the systems I designed are not working the way I thought they would.
- I'll take a 30-minute lunch at noon and go home around 6:30. I usually sneak in a few hours working early in the morning on weekends.
- I typically work 53-hour weeks, but when projects are due the weeks can get much longer.

Q: What do you like most about your job?
A: I like most aspects of my job but seeing a system I've designed go into production is the most satisfying part of it.

Q: What do you like least about your job?
A: The hardest part of my job is dealing with employees that don't try hard enough or make a lot of mistakes.

Q: What personal qualities do you find most valuable for this type of work?
A: Attention to detail. I can't stress that enough. Good engineers make vanishingly few engineering mistakes. A single engineering mistake can doom an entire space mission, just ask NASA about the Mars Climate Orbiter. This robotic space probe was lost in 1999 due to a ground-based computer software glitch.

Q: What advice do you have for students who might be interested in becoming robotics engineers?
A: Learn to be a good technical writer and a good technical speaker. These are both skills that can be learned and they are very different than speaking or writing for entertainment. In my experience, the best engineers are also the best communicators.

Other Jobs in Robotics

Aerospace engineering and operations technician
Assembler and fabricator
Computer and information systems manager
Computer hardware engineer
Computer programmer
Computer systems analyst
Corporate technology officer
Cost estimator
Database administrator
Electrical engineer
Electronics engineer
Industrial engineer
Industrial engineering technician
Industrial production manager
Information security analyst
Logistician
Machinist
Management analyst
Materials engineer
Mechanical engineer
Mechanical engineering technician
Network and computer systems administrator
Operations research analyst
Physicist
Quality control inspector
Software developer
Solderer
Statistician
Systems engineer
Welder

Editor's note: The online *Occupational Outlook Handbook* of the US Department of Labor's Bureau of Labor Statistics is an excellent source of information on jobs in hundreds of career fields, including many of those listed here. The *Occupational Outlook Handbook* may be accessed online at www.bls.gov/ooh.

Index